The Runes

in 9 minutes

Eoghan Odinsson

Visit my website at http://www.eoghanodinsson.com

ISBN 978-0-9878394-3-5

Published by: www.asgard-studios.com

SGARD STUDIOS
Content, Form, Function - Delivered

Cover Photograph by Elfya Amok Photography

http://elfyah.deviantart.com & http://elfyah.carbonmade.com

Library and Archives Canada Cataloguing in Publication

Odinsson, Eoghan, 1969-
    The runes in 9 minutes / Eoghan Odinsson.

Includes bibliographical references.
Issued also in an electronic format.
ISBN 978-0-9878394-3-5

    1. Runes. 2. Fortune-telling by runes. I. Title. II. Title:
Runes in nine minutes.

BF1891.R85O45 2012   133.3'3   C2012-900852-4

Also by the Author

Northern Lore - A Field Guide to the Northern Mind, Body & Spirit

Winner for Best New Age . Non-Fiction Book of 2011!

Northern Wisdom - The Havamal, Tao of the Vikings

Northern Plant Lore - A Field Guide to the Ancestral Use of Plants in Northern Europe

Dedication

I warmly dedicate this work to Freya Aswynn who has been my inspiration and guide to the Runes for many years. When I first discovered her books and CD's, they resonated with my spirit like no other author. She truly embodies the runes, lives the runes.

It's been my privilege the last couple of years to get to know her personally, and although we are separated by an ocean, I am proud to call her sister and friend.

ᛁ᛫ᚲᚨᚱᚹᛖᛗᛉ ᛫ᚦᛖᛗᛊᛖ

ᚱᚢᛏᛖᛊ᛫ᚠᛟᚱ

ᚠᚱᛖᛗᛊᚨ᛫ᚨᛊᚹᛦᚾᚾ

About the Author

Canadian born Eoghan Odinsson is an award winning journalist and author with a lifelong passion for the knowledge of our Northern forefathers – or "folk lore". Literally, the knowledge of our people.

Graduating from the University of Aberdeen in Scotland with his Masters of Science degree, he subsequently taught for the University, and was a dissertation advisor for graduate students.

In addition to his academic background, Eoghan also holds a Black Belt in Shito-Ryu Karate, and has taught Martial Arts in Canada and the USA.

Eoghan has just returned from a 10 year stretch working in the Washington D.C. area, and is now back in his native Ottawa Valley where he lives with his wife, son and three dogs.

Eoghan is a proud Professional Member of the Canadian Authors Association.

Table of Contents

Chapter 1 Introduction

The word runes, for many, conjures up images of Tolkien's "The Hobbit", with dwarves, dragons and magical rings; after reading the book, I remember fondly learning how to write my name in (what I would later learn were) Anglo-Saxon runes. At the time they seemed like fanciful characters, and I was delighted to use them purely for aesthetic reasons – sketching in my school notebooks and such. Little did I know that 1500 years earlier, my ancestors used them daily, not only for writing, but also for magical and divinatory purposes.

This book has been designed to get you working with the runes in under 9 minutes, and you can easily be doing that. Chapter 1 has everything you need to get started, and after that, you can do a little more research and reading as you feel you want to do.

.

The future is no more uncertain than the present.

—*Walt Whitman*

Chapter 2   Getting Started

Using the Runes is easy and fun, let's jump right in!

A 90 Second Guide

- Grab a sheet of writing paper, pen and scissors *(or copy the diagrams on the next page and scale it up a bit)*

- Draw 3 vertical columns on the paper (up and down), then Draw 8 rows. That will give you 24 Squares

- Draw the symbols for each of the 24 Runes, 1 per square on your paper.

- Cut up the paper into the 24 squares

- Put them in a hat, dish or whatever you have to mix them up in.

- Formulate a question in your mind, or an issue you need guidance on. Concentrate on that for 30 seconds...clear your mind of everything else.

- Close your eyes and randomly pick one of the slips of paper with the rune symbol on it. You may feel drawn or guided to pick one...but do so without looking.

- Open your eyes and look at the rune and reference it's meaning in Chapter 6. There is one page per rune.

- Now it's up to you to decide what this means in the context of your life.

Congratulations! You have just done your first rune reading! It really is that simple. The magic is figuring out what the rune means to you. That can be very complicated.

ᚠ	ᚺ	↑
ᚢ	ᛏ	ᛒ
ᚦ	ᛁ	ᛗ
ᚨ	ᛇ	ᛘ
ᚱ	ᛃ	ᛚ
ᚲ	ᛈ	◇
ᚷ	ᛉ	ᛞ
ᚹ	ᛊ	ᛜ

Chapter 3   Making Your Own Runes

Materials

The runes themselves can be made out of many things as highlighted earlier. Often their symbols are drawn on slips of paper – there are many sets of "rune cards" out there on the market. My personal belief is that the forces in the multiverse you are tapping into probably don't care what medium their counsel gets delivered on. I've even used computer generated rune readings with success.

I have two sets of runes. The first set I made when I was first drawn to the runes, and a more serious study of our Northern Lore - these were made from river stones. I carved the rune staves on them with a rotary tool, and stained them with a mixture of ochre, boiled linseed oil and a few drops of my blood.

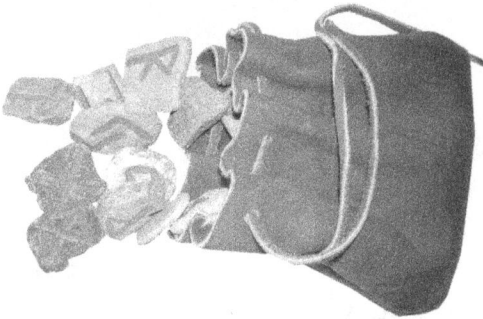

Author's Runes carved on river stone

The set I use daily though, comes from the branch of an apple tree whose limb was broken during a storm. I carved slips of wood from the branch, then burned the runes onto each slip using a wood burning tool. I then coated them with boiled linseed oil. I also made a bag of pigskin, with a leather draw cord ending in a Boar's tusk. Yours needn't be as elaborate, but for me the joy in creating something beautiful, useful, and charged with so much meaning, was a spiritual practice in itself. One I am reminded of every time I take out my bag of runes.

Author's Runes carved on slips of wood cut from an apple branch

Use of the Elder Futhark

There are many variants of the runic staves which we'll discuss in Chapter 5. In our exploration of the use of runes for divination, we'll work with the Elder Futhark. Some may wonder why I chose the Elder, rather than the Younger, which has a more recent history, and more numerous extant inscriptions etc. There are a few reasons for my preference, and that's all it is, simply a preference. People around the world work successfully with all the families of runes, but the Elder Futhark seems to resonate with me.

The runes are divided into groups called aetir – literally eights. The Elder Futhark are divided into three groups of eight runes; other families are grouped into three groups, but not necessarily of eight runes. To me this seems an inconsistency with the Elder Futhark. If our ancestors divided them into groups of eight, and we still use the term aetir, then why the change?

When contrasting the Elder versus Younger runic rows, I also noticed a significant difference in the scope of their interpretations that seemed to signify to me, a shift in the world view, or attitudes of our ancestors. For example the rune Kenaz in the Elder Futhark means Torch, and can symbolize light, learning and inspiration. It can also signify the energy of fire, in both negative and positive aspects. This description feels balanced to me. If we now look at the equivalent rune in the Younger Futhorc, Kaun, we see a marked difference in its meaning – Cancer, Ulcer. It seems to me to be a very negative rune. It's lost its balance in my view.

Other changes include the removal of Gebo, the rune for Gift, and of Wunjo, the rune for Joy. I'm speculating that perhaps due to the changes in conditions that drove our ancestors to go a-viking in the first place, they also began to have a more negative, and less balanced view of the world. In my own search for meaning, I'm looking for balance. To me, the Elder Futhark feels right. Let me add that I recognize that systems evolve, as the elder futhark did into the younger and others; perhaps for me choosing the elder runes, this is simply closing the loop on that evolution – coming full circle if you will.

Please don't let my preference dissuade you from using any of the different runic rows in your own work, I simply want to highlight my own rationale for choosing one over another.

Just a quick note, I will be using the commonly accepted reconstructed Germanic names for the runes.

My interest is in the future because I am going to spend the rest of my life there.

—Charles Kettering

Chapter 4 Quantum Physics is Wyrd!

A Chapter on Quantum Physics? Wrong Book? Nope…read on.

For those of you who are new to the Northern Traditions, *Wyrd* is somewhat like fate. The word *Wyrd* is cognate (related) to many words in the Germanic languages and roughly means "to come to pass, to become, to be due". Wyrd is an important concept when learning about the runes.

Wyrd is not your fate or destiny carved in stone, we are not trapped by Wyrd, but our lives are shaped by it. For example, suppose you were born with no legs. Would that mean you would be fated to never run a marathon? Certainly not. It would make it a big challenge, but with today's technology it could be overcome – via prosthetics for example.

So Wyrd sets us on a certain course, but we have the ability to alter course, and change our lives – so our forefathers believed.

My thoughts one day happened on Wyrd, and my belief in it. From time to time I like to consider what I "believe" in…..we all change, and sometimes it's good to re-examine old beliefs in light of new experience, evidence etc.

Here's where we get to the Scientific stuff (cover your ears if you must).

The Physics our grandfathers learned were heavily dependent on the works of Sir Isaac Newton – you know the guy who thought up gravity after being hit on the head by an apple. So we know that branch of physics as *Newtonian Physics*. I like Newtonian Physics; it's neat, tidy, and certain. You can calculate things, and know what to expect.

If the multiverse were governed purely by Newtonian Physics, then the Universe should be totally predictive...that is, if I had all the information, I could predict any event with 100% accuracy. So life would be pre-destined, which would contradict our understanding of Wyrd - which we can influence.

Hmmm....so do we throw out the concept of Wyrd in favour of Newtonian Physics? Not yet.

Quantum physics or mechanics, tells us that there is no certainty, only probability (things exist in multiple states simultaneously), there can be no prediction of a single outcome, all outcomes are viable, and do occur. So we likely have layers of realities - multiple universes, or the multiverse – a bubbly frothy foam of possibility.

So actions I take, according to Quantum Physics, will affect things in a way nobody can predict ahead of time. We can only talk about probable outcomes. So then my "fate" is not set in stone! My "Wyrd" is mine to manipulate, and even the Gods don't know where I'll end up! So use the runes – shape your life!

Chapter 5 How to Use Them

The most common way to use the runes today is the "drawing of lots" or picking runes to help guide us relating to some question. Typically a querent (the person with the question) will formulate the question, then draw runes from a bag. It could be a single rune, or several, as we'll see.

Odin Cast

This is the reading we did in the 90 Second Guide in Chapter 1, and is very common. I often draw a single rune, sometimes referred to as an Odin cast, when I want some relatively straightforward guidance to a particular question and would go through the following steps:

- Relax your mind and ensure you are in a calm state and free from distractions and negative influences

- Formulate the question in your mind e.g. "What will happen if I take that new job?"

- Focus on the question as you draw a single rune - pick one you feel guided to

- Place the rune down on a table or other surface

- Interpret the possible meaning of the rune in relation to the question you have posed – consult the meanings and associations that follow

Norn Cast

A second method can be used when you want more detailed guidance, and involve drawing three runes to provide a more complete picture of the influences on your question at hand. It is often referred to as a Norn cast, in reference to Urd, Verdandi and Skuld (representing past, present and future).

You would start the Norn cast in the same manner as the Odin cast, but would choose three runes, one at a time. Laying each down separately left to right. The first representing the past (Urd), the second representing the present (Verdandi) and the final rune representing the future, or potential outcomes (Skuld).

Urd   Verdandi   Skuld

Past   Present   Future

Once the three runes were laid, you would then analyze the meaning of each. The first rune represents the forces or influences in your past, the second indicates condition or influences in your present and the third hints at potential outcomes and directions – our ancestors did not believe the future was predetermined.

Celtic Cross

A third and more comprehensive reading, is known as a *Celtic Cross*. This is the type of spread that you might want to use if you have a very complex situation in front of you and want to do a careful analysis of all the factors and influences.

The pattern is named after the formation it resembles and uses six runes. Draw each rune, one at a time, and lay them out according to the diagram below. Once the runes are laid out, you can begin to do the detailed analysis. Use the guide below for each rune in the spread to determine how it's influencing your situation and consult the detailed meanings of the runes.

1) The root of the problem.

2) Where you should direct your energy.

3) Problems you're facing now.

4) What will help you overcome the problem?

5) What are you still lacking?

6) Outcome of the situation.

The future, according to some scientists, will be exactly like the past, only far more expensive.

—*John Sladek*

Chapter 6   How to Read Them

Each rune and it's meanings and associations have to be considered in the context of your life – which includes your past, present activity as well as considerations for the future.

Once you have drawn your rune(s), consult the descriptions of each rune. I've tried to provide the most common exoteric, as well as esoteric meanings associated with each rune (Per Thorsson, Aswynn, et al). Consider them carefully as you try to unlock the guidance you have been provided.

I've also provided the Anglo-Saxon rune poems for each. These may additionally have more subtle codified meanings for the runes.

"The Old English Rune Poem records stanzas for the twenty-nine-stave Old English Futhorc. This is especially valuable because it is a source for the lore of the staves of the Elder Futhark not present in the younger row."

- Edred Thorsson, Futhark

Name: Fehu

Meaning: Livestock, Wealth, Energy, Fertility, Creation

Phoenetic Value: F

Anglo-Saxon Rune Poem

Wealth is a comfort to all men,

Yet one must give it away freely,

If he wants to gain glory in the Lord's sight.

Name: Uruz

Meaning: The Aurochs, Health, Wisdom, Vital Strength

Phoenetic Value: U

Anglo-Saxon Rune Poem

The aurochs is proud and has great horns;

it is a very savage beast and fights with its horns;

a great ranger of the moors, it is a creature of mettle.

Name: Thurisaz

Meaning: Giant, Thorn, Destruction/ Defense

Phoenetic Value: TH

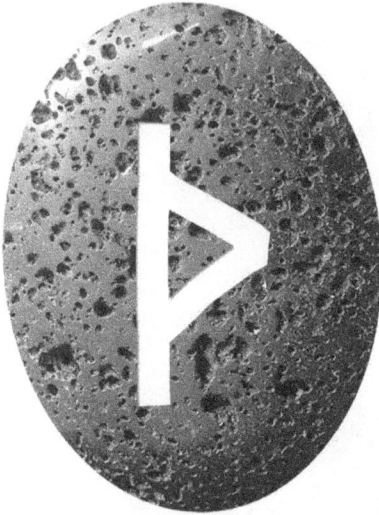

Anglo-Saxon Rune Poem

The thorn is exceedingly sharp,

an evil thing for any knight to touch,

uncommonly severe on all who sit among them.

Name: Ansuz

Meaning: A god (Odinn), Mouth, Song, Poetry, Inspiration, Knowledge

Phoenetic Value: A

Anglo-Saxon Rune Poem

The mouth is the source of all language,

a pillar of wisdom and a comfort to wise men,

a blessing and a joy to every knight.

Name: Raido

Meaning: Ride, Journey, a Path, Ritual, Rhythm

Phoenetic Value: R

Anglo-Saxon Rune Poem

Riding seems easy to every warrior while he is indoors

and very courageous to him who traverses the high-roads

on the back of a stout horse.

Name: Kenaz

Meaning: Torch, Enlightenment, Hearth, Controlled Energy, Creativity

Phoenetic Value: K (or hard C)

Anglo-Saxon Rune Poem

The torch is known to every living man by its pale, bright flame;

it always burns where princes sit within.

Name: **Gebo**

Meaning: Gift, Sacrifice, Hospitality

Phoenetic Value: G

Anglo-Saxon Rune Poem

Generosity brings credit and honour, which support one's dignity;

it furnishes help and subsistence

to all broken men who are devoid of aught else.

Name: Wunjo

Meaning: Joy, Hope, Well Being, Binding, Fellowship

Phoenetic Value: W or V

Anglo-Saxon Rune Poem

Bliss he enjoys who knows not suffering, sorrow nor anxiety,

and has prosperity and happiness and a good enough house.

Name: Hagalaz

Meaning: Hail, Transformation, Evolution, Destruction, Seed of Primal Life

Phoenetic Value: H

Anglo-Saxon Rune Poem

Hail is the whitest of grain;

it is whirled from the vault of heaven

and is tossed about by gusts of wind

and then it melts into water.

Name: Nauthiz

Meaning: Need, Deliverance from Distress, Resistance

Phoenetic Value: N

Anglo-Saxon Rune Poem

Trouble is oppressive to the heart;

yet often it proves a source of help and salvation

to the children of men, to everyone who heeds it betimes.

Name: Isa

Meaning: Ice, Preservation, Lack of Motion, Ego, Anti-Matter, Concentration

Phoenetic Value: I (like ee)

Anglo-Saxon Rune Poem

Ice is very cold and immeasurably slippery;

it glistens as clear as glass and most like to gems;

it is a floor wrought by the frost, fair to look upon.

Name: Jera

Meaning: Year, Harvest, Reward, Fruition

Phoenetic Value: J or Y

Anglo-Saxon Rune Poem

Summer is a joy to men, when God, the holy King of Heaven,

suffers the earth to bring forth shining fruits

for rich and poor alike.

to look upon.

Name: Eiwhaz

Meaning: Yew, World Tree, Vertical Cosmic Axis, Life / Death, Protection, Endurance

Phoenetic Value: E

Anglo-Saxon Rune Poem

The yew is a tree with rough bark,

hard and fast in the earth, supported by its roots,

a guardian of flame and a joy upon an estate.

30

Name: Pertho

Meaning: Dice Cup, Chance, Birth, Wyrd, Orlog, The Norns, Time

Phoenetic Value: P

Anglo-Saxon Rune Poem

Pertho is a source of recreation and amusement to the great,

where warriors sit blithely together in the banqueting-hall.

Name: Algiz

Meaning: Elk, Protection, Sanctuary, Life, Bifrost, Connection between gods and men

Phoenetic Value: Z

Anglo-Saxon Rune Poem

The Eolh-sedge is mostly to be found in a marsh;

it grows in the water and makes a ghastly wound,

covering with blood every warrior who touches it.

Name: Sowilo

Meaning: Sun, Guide, Goal and Path, Success, Honor

Phoenetic Value: S

Anglo-Saxon Rune Poem

The sun is ever a joy in the hopes of seafarers

when they journey away over the fishes' bath,

until the courser of the deep bears them to land.

Name: Teiwaz

Meaning: The God Tyr, Law, Justice, Victory, Self-Sacrifice, Spiritual Discipline

Phoenetic Value: T

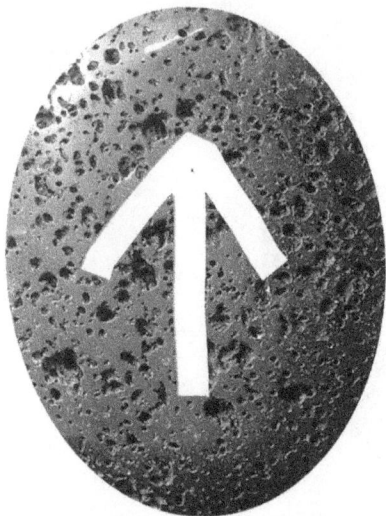

Anglo-Saxon Rune Poem

Teiwaz is a guiding star; well does it keep faith with princes;

it is ever on its course over the mists of night and never fails.

Name: Berkana

Meaning: Birch, Earth Mother, Renewal, Birth-Life-Death Cycle

Phoenetic Value: B

Anglo-Saxon Rune Poem

The poplar bears no fruit; yet without seed it brings forth suckers,

for it is generated from its leaves.

Splendid are its branches and gloriously adorned

its lofty crown which reaches to the skies.

Name: Ehwaz

Meaning: Horse, Fertility, Vehicle for Otherworldly Journeys, Trust, Loyalty, Legal Marriage

Phoenetic Value: E

Anglo-Saxon Rune Poem

The horse is a joy to princes in the presence of warriors.

A steed in the pride of its hoofs,

when rich men on horseback bandy words about it;

and it is ever a source of comfort to the restless.

Name: Mannaz

Meaning: Man, Humanity, Intelligence, Divine Structure, Self-Realization, Fulfillment

Phoenetic Value: M

Anglo-Saxon Rune Poem

The joyous man is dear to his kinsmen;

yet every man is doomed to fail his fellow,

since the Lord by his decree will commit the vile carrion to the earth

Name: Laguz

Meaning: Lake, Water, Life, Growth, Flow, Basic Energy, Source of Life

Phoenetic Value: L

Anglo-Saxon Rune Poem

The ocean seems interminable to men,

if they venture on the rolling bark

and the waves of the sea terrify them

and the courser of the deep heed not its bridle.

Name: Inguz

Meaning: The God Ingvi Frey, Potential Energy, Gestation, Seed

Phoenetic Value: NG

Anglo-Saxon Rune Poem

Ing was first seen by men among the East-Danes,

till, followed by his chariot,

he departed eastwards over the waves.

So the Heardingas named the hero.

Name: Dagaz

Meaning: Day, Light, Polarity, A Turning Point

Phoenetic Value: D

Anglo-Saxon Rune Poem

Day, the glorious light of the Creator, is sent by the Lord;

it is beloved of men, a source of hope and happiness to rich and poor,

and of service to all.

Name: Othila

Meaning: Property, Inheritance, Sacred Enclosure

Phoenetic Value: O

Anglo-Saxon Rune Poem

An estate is very dear to every man,

if he can enjoy there in his house

whatever is right and proper in constant prosperity.

The most depressing thing that can happen to a prophet is to be proved wrong. The next most distressing thing is to be proved right.

—*Aldous Huxley*

Chapter 7 Hafskjold Rune Casting

One small treasure I was given years ago, was the knowledge of Hafskjold rune casting. This was taught to me by my *Stav* instructor, Graham Butcher from the U.K.

Stav is a Mind-Body-Spirit System taught by Ivar Hafskjold. It uses runes and Norse Mythology in its teaching based on oral tradition preserved in his family.

In the 1990s, Ivar Hafskjold took on four personal apprentice students; Shaun Brassfield-Thorpe, Kolbjorn Märtens, David Watkinson and Graham Butcher. All contemporary Stav teachers belong to a teaching lineage directly from either Ivar Hafskjold and/or one of his first four students, each of whom are recognized as masters.

Stav resembles T'ai chi, with the student beginning with ritualized stances resembling the sixteen runes of the Younger Futhark.

A unique part of the Stav tradition is its method of rune casting. Stav uses the sixteen runes of the Younger futhork, but in creating their runes tiles, they utilize a method I've seen nowhere else.

Making the Runes

They start by cutting Twenty-Four tiles, then inscribing or carving the sixteen runes of the younger futhork three times over (starting on the front side of the twenty-four tiles, then turning them over). You end up with twenty-four runes tiles with the sixteen rune staves of the younger futhork carved on each side of the tiles, the whole runic row repeated three times.

The result is that when doing a three-rune spread such as the *Norn Cast*, you can get the same rune more than once, possibly, though unlikely, three times!

The lesson here is that it's possible that your past, present situation, and future actions could all be influenced by similar forces. I've used this method for seven years and have never drawn three of the same rune, but the possibility is there. Per quantum physics you must allow that anything is possible. As I said previously, quantum physics is Wyrd!

Top	1	2	3	4	5	6
Bottom						
Top	7	8	9	10	11	12
Bottom						
Top	13	14	15	16	17	18
Bottom						
Top	19	20	21	22	23	24
Bottom						

45

Younger Futhork Meanings

We use the runes in the Hafskjold Stav tradition in much the same way as the Elder Futhark runes. Typically I do either a one-rune draw or three-rune layout. If you want to try your hand at casting the runes of the Younger futhork in the Hafskjold tradition, here is a very concise list of their meanings, with a chart for each of the three groups, or aets. Refer to Graham Butcher's books on the runes for more detailed information.

To learn more about Stav and the Hafskjold tradition, please visit Graham Butcher's Ice & Fire Stav website at:

http://www.iceandfire.org.uk

FREY'S AETT

Rune	Name	Meaning	Norwegian Rune Poem
ᚠ	Fe	Portable wealth, riches	Wealth is a source of discord among kinsmen; the wolf lives in the forest.
ᚢ	Ur	Slag, Aurochs, Primal forces	Slag comes from bad iron; the reindeer often races over the frozen snow
ᚦ	Thor	Giant, Thorn, Protection	Giant causes anguish to women; misfortune makes few men cheerful.
ᚨ	As	Mouth, Beginnings, Wisdom	Estuary is the way of most journeys; but a scabbard is of swords.
ᚱ	Rei	Journey by Horseback, Travel, Transformation	Riding is said to be the worst thing for horses; Reginn forged the finest sword
ᚴ	Kreft	Ulcer, Cancer, Canker	Ulcer is fatal to children; death makes a corpse pale

HEIMDALL'S AETT

Rune	Name	Meaning	Norwegian Rune Poem
ᚼ	Hagl	Hail, Sudden Change	Hail is the coldest of grain; Christ created the world of old
ᚾ	Nod	Need, Crisis	Constraint gives scant choice; a naked man is chilled by the frost.
ᛁ	Isa	Ice, Frozen, Static	Ice we call the broad bridge; the blind man must be led
ᛅ	Ar	Year, Cycle, Harvest	Plenty is a boon to men; I say that Frothi was generous.
ᛋ	Sol	Sun, Light, Victory	Sun is the light of the world; I bow to the divine decree.

TYR'S AETT

Rune	Name	Meaning	Norwegian Rune Poem
ᛏ	Tyr	The god Tyr, War, Justice, Sacrifice	Tyr is a one-handed god; often has the smith to blow.
ᛒ	Bjork	Birch, Re-Birth, New Beginnings, Female Energies, Family	Birch has the greenest leaves of any shrub; Loki was fortunate in his deceit.
ᛘ	Mann	Mankind, The Moon	Man is an augmentation of the dust; great is the claw of the hawk.
ᛚ	Laug	Lake, Water, Fluidity, Wealth	A waterfall is a River, which falls from a mountainside; but ornaments are of gold.
ᛣ	Yr	The Yew Tree, Male Energies, Archery	Yew is the greenest of trees in winter; it is wont to crackle when it burns.

Chapter 8   History of the Runes

For those of you who want to dig in a bit deeper, this chapter will explore a little of the esoteric (magical) and exoteric (mundane) aspects of the Runes.

Much of the esoteric uses of the runes have been re-created in modern times with inspiration from documented practices of the North, and borrowing some bits and pieces from other cultures, such as the Chinese I-Ching, and European Tarot. Our Lore is a living organism which evolves over time. You too will influence the evolution of that lore.

Divination

Our forefathers had a complex, and sophisticated tradition relating to the spiritual aspects of life; in addition to a wide ranging pantheon of deities, they practiced methods to divine the future and make decisions, connect with the spirits in the other worlds, and take journeys beyond the realm of Midgard.

There is evidence that runes historically served purposes of magic in addition to being a writing system. This is the case from earliest epigraphic evidence of the Roman to Germanic Iron Age, and in medieval sources, notably the Poetic Edda, which mentions "victory runes" to be carved on a sword, "some on the grasp and some on the inlay, and name Tyr twice."

Tacitus, the Roman historian, wrote the earliest known detailed description of Runic divination.

Their method of divining by lots is exceedingly simple. From a tree which bears fruit they cut a twig, and divide it into two small pieces. These they distinguish by so many several marks, and throw them at random and without order upon a white garment. Then the Priest of the community, if for the public the lots are consulted, or the father of a family about a private concern, after he has solemnly invoked the Gods, with eyes lifted up to heaven, takes up every piece thrice, and having done thus forms a judgment according to the marks before made. - Tacitus, Germania (98 CE)

While there is no clear-cut evidence that the "marks" referred to by Tacitus were Runes, this would seem probable.

Historical Origins

Rūn – Old English, meaning secret

So what are Runes? A runic row is a form of alphabet, which itself is a standardized set of letters — basic written symbols or graphemes - each of which roughly represents a phoneme in a spoken language, either as it exists now, or as it was in the past. Still with me?

The runes were used to write various Germanic languages prior to the adoption of the Latin alphabet, and later for specialized purposes. The Scandinavian variants are also known as futhork (or fuþork, derived from their first six letters of the alphabet: F, U, Þ, O, R, and K); the Anglo-Saxon variant is futhork (due to sound changes undergone in Old English).

The earliest runic inscriptions date from around 150 CE, and the characters were generally replaced by the Latin alphabet along with Christianization by around 700 CE in central Europe, and by around 1100 CE in Northern Europe; however, the use of runes persisted for specialized purposes in Northern Europe, longest in rural Sweden, until the early twentieth century - used mainly for decoration such as on Runic calendars.

The three best-known runic rows, and their approximate years of common usage are:

- **Elder Futhark** (around 150 to 800 CE),

- **Anglo-Saxon Futhorc** (400 to 1100 CE),

- **Younger Futhork** (800–1100 CE).

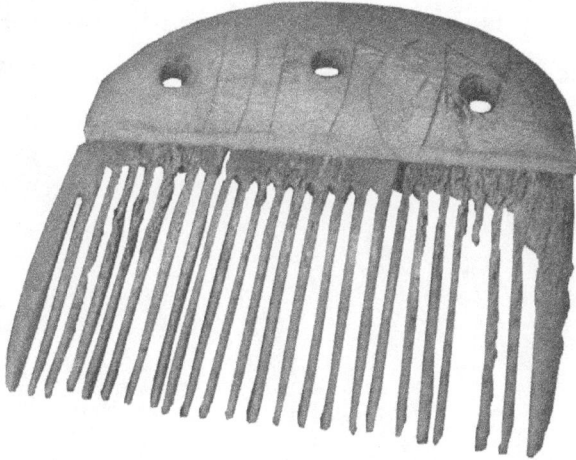

A comb made of antler from around 150 to 200 CE and was found in Vimose on the island of Funen, Denmark. The Elder Futhark inscription reads "Harja", a male name. This is the oldest known runic inscription. The comb is housed at the National Museum of Denmark.

Elder Futhark

The Elder Futhark is the oldest form of the runic row, used by Germanic tribes for Northwest Germanic and Migration period Germanic people of the 2nd to 8th centuries for inscriptions on artifacts such as jewellery, amulets, tools, weapons and runestones. In Scandinavia, the script was simplified to the Younger Futhork from the late 8th century, while the Anglo-Saxons and

51

Frisians extended the Futhark which eventually became the Anglo-Saxon futhorc.

Unlike the Younger Futhork, which remained in use until modern times, the knowledge of how to read the Elder Futhark was forgotten, and it wasn't until 1865 that the Norwegian scholar Sophus Bugge managed to decipher it.

Elder Rune	Germanic Name	Meaning
ᚠ	Fehu	Cattle, Portable Wealth
ᚢ	Uruz	Aurochs
ᚦ	Thurisaz	Giant
ᚨ	Ansuz	A god
ᚱ	Raido	Riding
ᚲ	Kenaz	Torch, light
ᚷ	Gebo	Gift
ᚹ	Wunjo	Joy
ᚺ	Hagalaz	Hail
ᚾ	Nauthiz	Need
ᛁ	Isa	Ice
ᛃ	Jera	Year, harvest
ᛇ	Eihwaz	Yew
ᛈ	Pertho	Birth, chance
ᛉ	Algiz	Protection
ᛊ	Sowilo	Sun
ᛏ	Teiwaz	the god Tyr
ᛒ	Berkana	Birch (or Poplar)
ᛖ	Ehwaz	Horse
ᛗ	Mannaz	Man
ᛚ	Laguz	Water, lake
◇	Inguz	the god Freyr
ᛞ	Dagaz	Day
ᛟ	Othila	Inherited land

The Elder Futhark consists of 24 runes that are arranged in three groups of eight; each group is referred to as an Ætt or aettir. The earliest known sequential listing of the full set of 24 runes dates to around 400

AD and is found on the Kylver Stone in Gotland, Sweden (pictured below).

Each rune most probably had a name, chosen to represent the sound of the rune itself. The names are, however, not directly attested for the Elder Futhark themselves. Reconstructed names in Proto-Germanic have been produced, based on the names given for the runes in the later alphabets attested in the rune poems and the linked names of the letters of the Gothic alphabet.

Anglo-Saxon Futhorc

The Anglo-Saxon Futhorc was descended from the Elder Futhark of 24 runes and contained between 26 and 33 characters. It was used probably from the fifth century onward, for recording Old English and Old Frisian.

The front panel of the 7th century Franks Casket, depicting the Germanic legend of Weyland Smith and containing a riddle in Anglo-Saxon runes. Note how runes are written left to right at the top, and right to left at the bottom.

There are competing theories as to the origins of the Anglo-Saxon futhorc. One theory proposes that it was developed in Frisia and from there spread later to England. Another holds that runes were first introduced to England from Scandinavia where the futhorc was modified and then exported to Frisia.

The early futhorc was identical to the Elder Futhark except for the split of ᚠ a into three variants ᚪ āc, ᚫ æsc and ᚩ ōs, resulting in 26 runes. The earliest ᚩ ōs rune is found on the 5th century Undley bracteate. ᚪ āc was introduced later, in the 6th century. The double-barred ᚻ hægl characteristic for continental inscriptions is first attested as late as 698, on St. Cuthbert's coffin; before that, the single-barred Scandinavian variant was used.

ANGLO SAXON FUTHORC

| feoh · f "wealth" | ur · u "cattle" | þorn · þ "thorn" | os · o "mouth" | rad · r "ride" | cen · c "torch" | ȝiefu · ȝ "gift" | pynn · p "joy" | hæȝl · h "hail" |

| nyd · n "need" | is · i "ice" | jear · j "year" | eeoh · eo "yew" | peorð · p "game" | eolxecȝ · x "elk-sedge" | siȝel · s "sun" | tyr · t "tyr" | beorc · b "birch" |

| eoh · e "horse" | man · m "man" | lagu · l "lake" | ing · ŋ "Ing" | œðel · œ "estate" | dæȝ · d "day" | ac · a "oak" | æsc · æ "ash" |

| yr · y "bow" | ear · ea "earth" | iar · ia "serpent" | kalc · k | kalc · kk "chalice" | gar · g "spear" | cpeorð · cp "fire" | stan · st "stone" |

In England the futhorc was further extended to 28 and finally to 33 runes, and runic writing in England became closely associated with the Latin scriptoria from the time of Anglo-Saxon Christianization in the 7th century. The Thames scramasax (next page) is a 9th century weapon, recovered from the Thames at Battersea, London. It bears a Futhorc inscription. The row of 28 runes; this is the only known epigraphical example of the 28 Anglos-Saxon futhorc row. In addition to the futhorc, the name Beagnoþ is inscribed:

ᛒᛏᚷᚾᚨᚠᚦ

The futhorc started to be replaced by the Latin alphabet from around the 9th century. In some cases, texts would be written in the Latin alphabet but runes would be used in place of the word it represented, and the runes þorn (Þ, þ) and wynn (Ƿ, ƿ, ƿ) came to be used as extensions of the Latin alphabet. By the Norman Conquest of 1066 CE it was very rare and disappeared altogether shortly thereafter. From at least five centuries of use, fewer than 200 artifacts bearing futhorc inscriptions have survived.

The Anglo-Saxon rune poem lists the following character and names:

ᚠ feoh, ᚢ ur, ᚦ thorn, ᚩ os, ᚱ rad, ᚳ cen, ᚷ gyfu, ᚹ wynn, ᚻ haegl, ᚾ nyd, ᛁ is, ᛄ ger, ᛇ eoh, ᛈ peordh, ᛉ eolh, ᛋ sigel, ᛏ tir, ᛒ beorc ᛖ eh, ᛗ mann, ᛚ lagu, ᛝ ing, ᛟ ethel, ᛞ daeg, ᚪ ac, ᚫ aesc, ᚣ yr, ᛡ ior, ᛠ ear.

The expanded alphabet features the additional letters ᛢ cweorth, ᛣ calc, ᛤ cealc and ᛥ stan- these additional letters have only been found in manuscripts. Feoh, þorn, and sigel stood for [f], [þ] and [s] in most environments, but voiced to [v], [ð], and [z] between vowels or voiced consonants. Gyfu and wynn stood for the letter yogh and wynn, which became [g] and [w] in Middle English.

Younger Futhork

The Younger Futhork, also called Scandinavian runes, is a reduced form of the Elder Futhark, consisting of only 16 characters, in use from ca. 800 CE. The reduction, paradoxically, happened at the same time as phonetic changes led to a greater number of different phonemes in the spoken language, when Proto-Norse evolved into Old Norse.

YOUNGER FUThORK

fe - f	ur- u	thor- th	as- os	rei - r	kreft - k
"Cattle"	"Slag"	"thunder, thorn"	"mouth"	"wheel, road"	"canker"

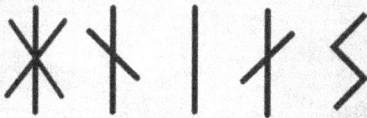

hagl - h	nod - n	is - i (ee)	ar - a	sol - s
"hail"	"need"	"ice"	"year"	"sun"

tyr- t	bjork - b	mann - m	laug - l	yr- y,j
"war, justice"	"birch"	"mankind"	"water"	"yew tree"

Thus, the language included distinct sounds and minimal pairs which were not separate in writing. Also, since the writing custom avoided having the same rune twice in consecutive order, the spoken distinction between long and short vowels were not retained in writing, either. The only real reason for using the same rune consecutively, would be when it represented different sounds following each other. Usage of the Younger Futhork is found in Scandinavia and Viking Age settlements abroad, probably in use from the 9th century onward. While the Migration Period Elder Futhark had been an actual "secret" known only to a literate elite, with only some 350 surviving inscriptions, literacy in the Younger Futhork became widespread in Scandinavia, as witnessed by the great number of Runestones (some 6,000), sometimes inscribed with almost casual notes.

The Younger Futhork became known in Europe as the "alphabet of the Norsemen", and was studied in the interest of trade and diplomatic contacts, referred to as Abecedarium Nordmannicum in Frankish Fulda (possibly by Walahfrid Strabo) and *ogam lochlannach* "Ogham of the Scandinavians" in the Book of Ballymote.

The Younger Futhork is divided into long-branch (Danish) and short-twig (Swedish and Norwegian) runes. The difference between the two versions has been a matter of controversy. A general opinion is that the difference was functional, i.e. the long-branch runes were used for documentation on stone, whereas the short-branch runes were in everyday use for private or official messages on wood. In addition the **Hälsinge Runes** (staveless runes, ca. 900–1200), **Middle Age runes** (ca. 1100–1500) and the Latinized **Dalecarlian futhark** (ca. 1500–1910) were developed out of the Younger futhark.

The Icelandic and Norwegian rune poems list 16 runes, with the stave names:

ᚠ fe ("wealth"), ᚢ ur ("iron"/"rain"), ᚦ Thurs ("giant"), ᚬ As/Oss, ᚱ reidh ("ride"), ᚴ kaun ("ulcer"), ᚼ hagall ("hail"), ᚾ naudhr/naud ("need"), ᛁ is/iss ("ice"), ᛆ ar ("plenty"), ᛋ sol ("sun"), ᛏ Tyr, ᛒ bjarkan/bjarken ("birch"), ᛘ madhr/madr ("man"), ᛚ logr/log ("water"), ᛦ yr ("yew").

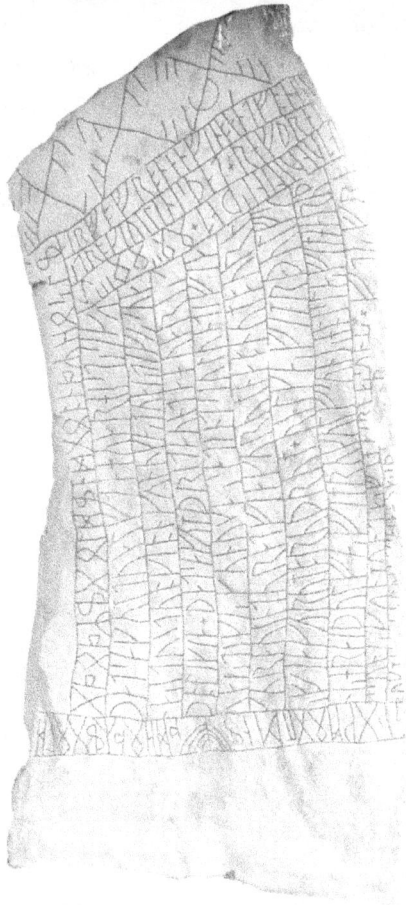

An inscription using cipher runes, the Elder Futhark and the Younger Futhark, on the 9th century Rök Runestone in Sweden.

There are no unnatural or supernatural phenomena, only very large gaps in our knowledge of what is natural . . . . We should strive to fill those gaps of ignorance.

—*Edgar d. Mitchell, Apollo 14 Astronaut*

Chapter 9 Further Study

Here is a short list of books I would recommend studying:

1. *"Northern Mysteries & Magick"* by Freya Aswynn. This is my all time favorite book on the Runes, and covers the esoteric aspects in great detail.

2. *"The Rune Primer - A Down-to-Earth Guide to the Runes"* by Sweyn Plowright. This is an incredible little tome, jam packed with good information on the runes, with no needless fluff.

3. *" FUTHARK - A Handbook of Rune Magic "* by Edred Thorsson. Edred was really the first expert to do serious and comprehensive research on the runes.

Of course everything in the bibliography is good, but the shortlist above will take you very far!

I really hope you enjoyed this little book - come and visit me on Facebook and we can chat about the runes! www.facebook.com/EoghanOdinsson

Head over to my website and find free FONT downloads for the different Runic Rows described here in the book.

http://www.eoghanodinsson.com/free-downloads.htm

Those who don't look forward remain behind.

—*Anonymous*

Bibliography

A. Craig Gibson, E. (1859). *Transactions of the Historic Society of Lancashire and Cheshire, Volume 11.* Liverpool: Historic Society of Lancashire and Cheshire.

Antonsen, E. H. (2002). *Runes and Germanic linguistics.* New York: Mouton de Gruyter.

Arthur, R. G. (2002). *English-Old Norse Dictionary.* Cambridge: In parentheses Publications.

Aswynn, F. (2002). *Northern Mysteries & Magick.* St.Paul: Llewellyn Publications.

Bonweits, I. (1989). *Real Magic.* York Beach: Samuel Weiser, Inc.

Davidson, H. E. (1990). *Gods and Myths of Northern Europe.* London: Penguin Books.

Davidson, H. E. (1999). *Myths and Symbols in Pagan Europe.* Syracuse: Syracuse University Press.

Delaney, F. (1991). *Legends of the Celts.* New York: Sterling Publishing Co., Inc.

Foster, M. H., & Cummings, A. M. (1922). *Asgard Stories - Tales from Norse Mythology.* Boston: Silver, Burdett and Company.

Guerber, H. A. (1895). *Myths of northern lands.* New York: American Book Company.

Gundarsson, K. (2006). *Our Troth: History and Lore (Volume 1).* BookSurge Publishing.

Larrington, C. (1999). *The Poetic Edda.* New York: Oxford University Press.

Lindow, J. (2001). Norse Mythology - A guide to the Gods, Heroes, Rituals and Beliefs. New York: Oxford University Press.

Little, E. L. (2004). National Audobon Society Field Guide to North American Trees. New York: Alfred A. Knopf, Inc.

Lloyd, J. (1892). *Elixirs and Flavoring Extracts*. New York: William Wood & Company.

Logan, F. D. (2005). *The Vikings in History*. New York: Routledge.

Looijenga, T. (2003). *Texts & contexts of the oldest Runic inscriptions*. Leiden: Brill Academic Publishers.

Page, R. (1999). Runes and runic inscriptions: collected essays on Anglo-Saxon and Viking runes. Boydell Press.

Paxson, D. L. (2005). Taking Up the Runes - A Complete Guide to Using Runes in Spels, Rituals, Divination, and Magic. San Franciso: Red Wheel/Weiser, LLC.

Pennick, N. (Boston). Magical Alphabets: The Secrets and Significance of Ancient Scripts -- Including Runes, Greek, Ogham, Hebrew and Alchemical Alphabets. 1992: Red Wheel / Weiser.

Pennick, N. (2002). *Practical Magic in the Northern Tradition*. Loughborough: Thoth Publications.

Pennick, N. (1992). *Rune Magic*. London: The Aquarian Press.

Peschel, L. (1999). *A Practical Guide to the Runes*. St. Paul: Llewellyn Publications.

Pitt, R. J. (1893). *The Tragedy of the Norse Gods*. London: T. Fisher Unwin.

Plowright, S. (2006). The Rune Primer - A Down-to-Earth Guide to the Runes. Lulu.

Rossman, D. ". (2005). The Northern Path - Norse Myths and Legends Retold....and What They Reveal. Chapel Hill: Seven Paws Press.

Spurkland, T. (2009). *Norwegian runes and runic inscriptions*. Rochester: Boydell Press.

Thorpe, B. (1852). Northern Mythology, Comprising the Popular Traditions and Superstitions of Scandinavia, Norther Germany, and The Netherlands: Volume I. Northern Mythology. London: Edward Lumley.

Thorpe, B. (1851). Northern Mythology, Comprising the Popular Traditions and Superstitions of Scandinavia, Norther Germany, and The Netherlands: Volume II. Scandinavian Popular Traditions and Superstitions. London: Edward Lumley.

Thorpe, B. (1852). Northern Mythology, Comprising the Popular Traditions and Superstitions of Scandinavia, Norther Germany, and The Netherlands: Volume III. North German and Netherlandish Popular Traditions and Superstitions. London: Edward Lumley.

Thorpe, B. (1851). Northern Mythology, Comprising the Principal Popular Traditions and Superstitions of Scandinavia, North Germany, and the Netherlands. Volume 1. London: Edward Lumley.

Thorsson, E. (1984). *FUTHARK - A Handbook of Rune Magic*. York Beach: Samuel Weiser Inc.

Thorsson, E. (2005). *Northern Magic - Rune Mysteries and Shamanism*. St. Paul: Llewellyn Publications.

Thorsson, E. (1990). Rune Might: Secret Pratices of the German Rune Magicians. St. Paul: Llewellyn Publications.

Thorsson, E. (1990). *Runelore - A Handbook of Esoteric Runology.* York Beach: Samuel Weiser, Inc.

Thorsson, E. (1994). *The Truth About Teutonic Magic.* St. Paul: Llewellyn.

Wodening, S. (2006). Germanic Magic - A Basic Primer on Galdor, Runes, Spa, and Herbs. Little Elm: Miercinga Rice.

Young, J. I. (1954). *the Prose Edda.* Los Angeles: University of California Press.

Also by Eoghan Odinsson

Northern Wisdom:

The Havamal, Tao of the Vikings

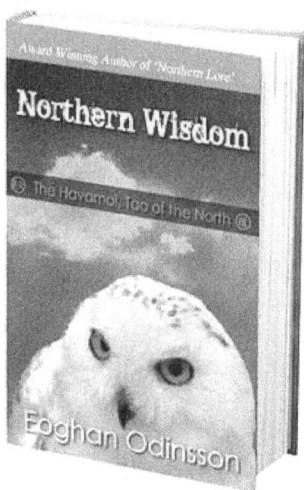

The Orient has long shared its ancient wisdom, and so now do the Northmen.

Northern Wisdom presents ancient Viking parables and knowledge in a delightfully accessible modern format.

Combining Teachings on par with Buddha, Sun-Tzu, Myamoto Musashi, Nicollo Machiavelli & Lao Tzu, The Havamal sheds light on forgotten lore of the dark ages.

In the days of the shield-wall, there yet lived poets, scribes and philosophers.

In Northern Wisdom you will:

- Journey through the Mundane and the Mystical passages of the Havamal
- Discover the famed Hospitality of the Northmen
- Learn Maxims for respectable conduct
- Develop the Leadership traits of Heroes
- Explore tips for safe travel in Dark Ages Europe
- Uncover lessons for the bravest Warriors
- Share in the secrets of Odin's Love Quests
- Tap into the power of Viking Magic

https://www.createspace.com/3711599

Save 15% - Use Coupon Code: **E8GSAJTG** When checking out

Northern Lore

A Field Guide to the Northern Mind, Body & Soul

Winner of the Global eBook Award for Best *New Age / Non-Fiction* Book in 2011 !

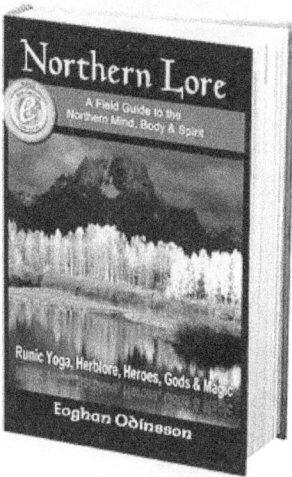

Northern Lore is a Field Guide to the Northern Mind-Body-Spirit, and will help you re-discover the Folk-Lore & Traditions of North Western Europe, and acquaint you with modern practices inspired by that lore.

In today's exciting cosmopolitan society, we tend to discard the old in favor of the new; and while discovering new traditions is a wonderful experience, it's important to also reflect on the traditions that have shaped our culture, and see where they've taken us.

In Northern Lore you will:

- Practice "Runic Yoga" for Health and Well Being
- Learn Ancient Herblore for Holistic Healing
- Meet your Animal Spirit Guide, or Fylgia
- Discover Lost Meaning in the Days of the Week
- Explore Modern Holidays & connections to Ancestral Festivals
- Unlock the Mysteries of the Runes
- Sample Viking and Anglo-Saxon cuisine

https://www.createspace.com/3451960/

Save 15% - Use Coupon Code: **E8GSAJTG** When checking out

Northern Plant Lore

A Field Guide to the Ancestral Use of Plants in Northern Europe

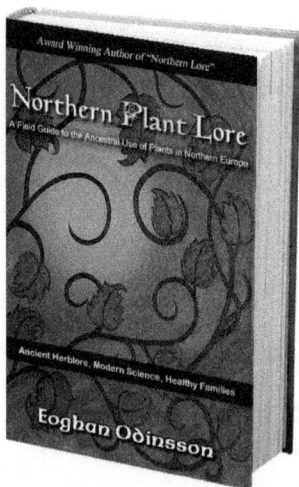

Over a thousand years ago our Anglo-Saxon ancestors used willow bark to treat headaches; modern pharmaceutical companies use the same basic ingredient - salicin.

Our folk boiled the bark in holy water and added a few other unnecessary ingredients, but they had a basic treatment that worked a millennia ago! And they called this the Dark Ages? Northern Plant Lore explores the plants and herbs used by our ancestors for medicinal purposes, and compares them to the list of plant and herbs proven effective by modern medical science. Not every plant they used worked, but Northern Plant Lore will show you which ones did, and how you can use them today.

In Northern Plant Lore you will:

- Discover Ancient Viking & Anglo-Saxon Remedies Supported by Modern Science
- Grow your own medicinal herbs and plants
- Create remedies at home with the same basis as modern pharmaceuticals
- Know exactly whats going into your body when you take an herbal remedy
- Cross reference ancient cures to modern science
- Browse ailments cross referenced to plants and treatments

https://www.createspace.com/3799295
Save 15% - Use Coupon Code: **E8GSAJTG** When checking out

Runic Notebook:

(Carry this book with you and make notes about your Rune readings on a daily basis in the 9 blank pages.)